DISCOVER SCIENCE
ACTION

Kim Taylor

Chrysalis Education

DISCOVER ● SCIENCE

Contents

US Publication copyright © 2003 Chrysalis Education
International copyright reserved in all countries.
No part of this book may be reproduced in any form
without written permission from the publisher.

Distributed in the United States by
Smart Apple Media
1980 Lookout Drive
North Mankato, Minnesota 56003

Copyright © Chrysalis Books PLC
Text © Kim Taylor Times Four Publishing Ltd
Photographs © Kim Taylor and Jane Burton
(except where credited elsewhere)

ISBN 1-93233-372-0
Library of Congress Control Number 2003102580

Designed by Robin Wright, Times Four Publishing Ltd

Illustrated by Guy Smith

Science advisers: Debbie Wright, Senior Lecturer,
Le Saint Union, Southampton
Richard Oels, Warden Park School,
Cuckfield, Sussex

Printed in Hong Kong

About this book

This book is about movement. It tells you how we start moving, what happens when we turn, leap and stop. You can find out about the fastest known thing and things that are so slow that you can hardly notice them moving. There are action photographs on every page which show how animals crawl, walk and jump, how birds fly and glide, and how fish swim.

There are simple experiments which are fun to do and which can help you find out more about the different kinds of movement. You can test your reactions, find out how fast you can run, and even hold water in an open container which is upside down! There are things for you to make, such as gliders, boats, and even a frog that jumps!

There are also lots of interesting facts about movement. Did you know that the first hang glider flew over 600 years ago, or that a feather and a stone can fall at the same speed? What is the fastest animal in the world, the longest skid mark ever made, the furthest distance ever walked? This book gives the answers to these questions and many more.

CAUTION: You may need to ask an adult to help with the cutting in the experiments which require the use of scissors or a knife.

Starting off

When an animal starts off it needs something solid to push against. Sprinters use starting blocks fixed to the ground to give them a strong push forward when the race starts.

To start anything moving takes a lot of **energy**. Heavy things are more difficult to get started than light things. But once something is moving, you need much less energy to keep it going at a steady speed.

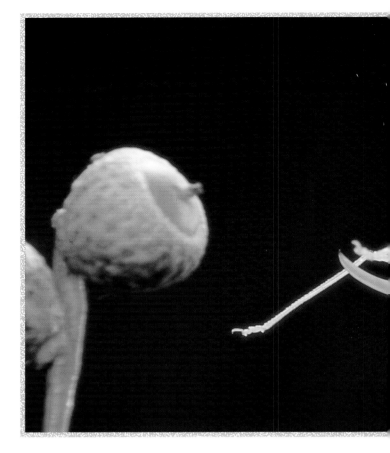

Oak-bush cricket

This oak-bush cricket has pushed off with its hind legs, using the solid acorn on the left as a starting block.

Falling apple

Gravity is a force which pulls everything to the ground. When the apple drops off the branch, gravity makes it fall faster and faster. This is called **acceleration**.

Cycling

When you start off on a bicycle you have to push hard against the pedals to get moving. Once you have got moving it is much easier to keep going at a steady speed.

Action experiment

PUSH OFF!

This experiment shows that animals and objects get off to a better start by pushing against something firm or solid.

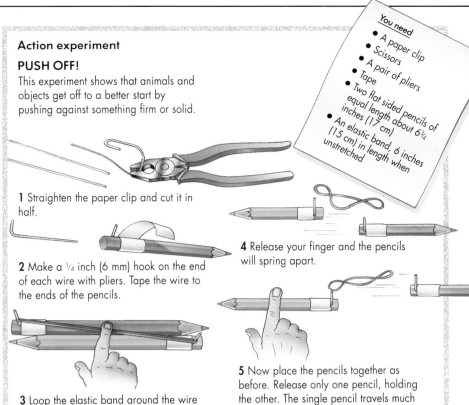

You need
- A paper clip
- Scissors
- A pair of pliers
- Tape
- Two flat sided pencils of equal length about 6¾ inches (17 cm)
- An elastic band, 6 inches (15 cm) in length when unstretched

1 Straighten the paper clip and cut it in half.

2 Make a ¼ inch (6 mm) hook on the end of each wire with pliers. Tape the wire to the ends of the pencils.

3 Loop the elastic band around the wire hooks and hold the pencils together with their ends level.

4 Release your finger and the pencils will spring apart.

5 Now place the pencils together as before. Release only one pencil, holding the other. The single pencil travels much further because it has something firm to push against.

Cycling is easier than running. When you run, your feet stop moving each time they hit the ground and then have to start off again quickly. Starting your feet moving at each stride uses energy and makes running hard work.

Did you know?

In a **vacuum**, which is a space without air, a stone and a feather fall at the same speed. This is because there is no air to slow down the fall of the feather.

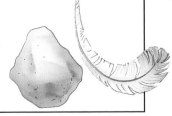

Moving

Everything on the earth moves – rocks, mountains, plants and animals. Some movements are so slow that you can hardly notice them, while others happen in a flash! The fastest known thing is light. It only takes about a second for light to reach the moon from the earth. Other things are much slower. In some places the ocean floor splits apart about the width of your hand each year. A slug takes a minute to travel the same distance. It takes a plant only about a week to grow as much as you do in a year.

Speed is the distance something travels in a fixed time. A car moving at 50 miles (80 km) an hour takes one hour to travel that distance.

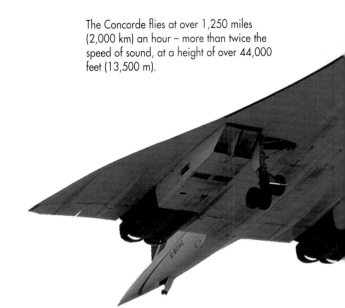

The Concorde flies at over 1,250 miles (2,000 km) an hour – more than twice the speed of sound, at a height of over 44,000 feet (13,500 m).

When a green woodpecker flies fast its wings are swept back, like the Concorde's, to cut down air resistance.

Shape and speed

The fastest birds, such as swifts and hawks, and planes, such as the Concorde, have swept-back wings to reduce air resistance. But resistance from water is even greater. Fast fish have slim, smooth bodies and racing boats have **streamlined** hulls to cut down the water resistance.

Action experiment
HOW FAST?

This experiment shows you how to find out the speed you travel over a certain distance.

1 Measure a distance of about 20 yards (or 20 m). Mark each end with chalk, or by placing sticks on the pavement.

2 Time how long it takes a friend to walk, then run the 20 yards (or 20 m).

To find your speed

Suppose it took you 10 seconds to walk the 20 yards (20 m). To find your speed, divide the distance by the time you take. This will give your speed in yards (m) per second

$$\frac{20}{10} = 2 \text{ yards (m) per second}$$

Swift and slow

20 feet (6 m) per hour

22 miles (36 km) per hour

70 miles (112 km) per hour

105 miles (170 km) per hour

The fastest animal in the air is the spine-tailed swift. Fastest on land is the cheetah. In a 220 yard (200 m) race, the swift would finish in 4 seconds, a cheetah in 6 seconds. The fastest sprinter would take more than 19 seconds, and a snail more than 33 hours to finish!

Curving through the air

Did you know?

The further away an archer stands, the higher above the target the arrow must be aimed. This is to allow for the arrow's trajectory.

If you threw a ball in outer space it would keep going in a straight line, at the same speed forever. Back on Earth, what goes up must come down. This is because on Earth there is a force called **gravity** which pulls everything to the ground (see page 4).

When you throw a ball it goes up into the air because of the force you use when you throw it. Then it starts to curve as gravity pulls it back to Earth. The imaginary downwards curve that an object makes in the air is called its **trajectory**.

The lifeline helps you to see the spider's trajectory.

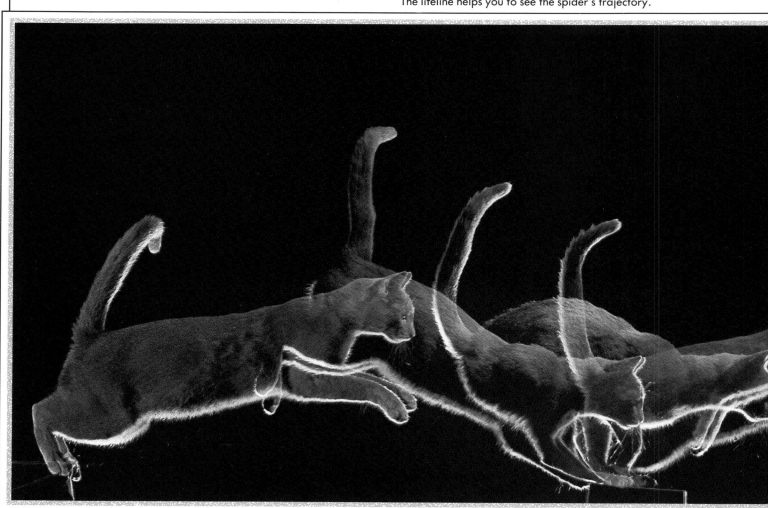

Jumping spider

Jumping spiders use a strand of web as a lifeline when they jump or pounce on their prey. This spider missed its landing pad!

Action experiment

TRACK THE CURVE!

This experiment shows that the shape of a trajectory depends on how an object is thrown.

1 Tape the paper to the board. Prop it up with a brick. Spread paper towels or newspapers under the boards to catch the marble.

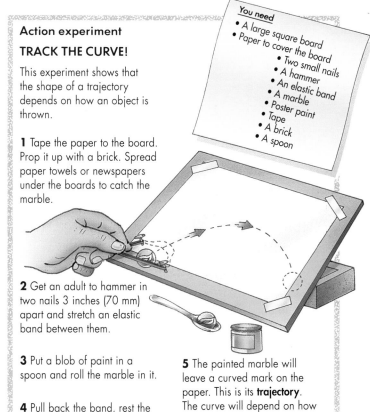

2 Get an adult to hammer in two nails 3 inches (70 mm) apart and stretch an elastic band between them.

3 Put a blob of paint in a spoon and roll the marble in it.

4 Pull back the band, rest the marble on it. Slowly release the band.

5 The painted marble will leave a curved mark on the paper. This is its **trajectory**. The curve will depend on how fast and at what angle the marble moves.

A cat uses its tail to help it balance when it is leaping.

Cat curve

Cats often bound along when they are in a hurry. A leaping cat is pulled downwards by gravity and so it has to jump upwards as well as forwards. This picture shows the cat's trajectory as it leaps through the air.

9

Reacting

You can blink your eye in a fraction of a second to avoid dust or sand. Yet some **reactions** need to be learned. If someone throws you a ball, you may see it coming, yet fail to catch it because your reactions are too slow. When a ball is thrown at you, your eyes send the picture to your brain. In turn, your brain sends messages through your nerves to your arms, hands and fingers to catch the ball. This takes time, because nerves cannot carry messages very quickly. It takes your fingers at least one eighth of a second to react to messages from the brain. Compare this with computers which can react in a few billionths of a second!

Swatting a fly

Here's what happens if you try to swat a fly on the back of your hand. As you move your right hand, the fly sees it, but does not recognize it as a danger. Suddenly you smack your hand down on the fly, feeling sure you must have squashed it. But the fly can react to danger in one hundredth of a second and easily escapes.

The fly lands on the back of your hand.

The fly reacts to danger in one hundred

It takes a car driver time to react to danger. A car going at 50 miles (80 km) an hour will travel 18 yards (16 m) by the time the driver's foot has hit the brakes. The car will travel much farther before stopping.

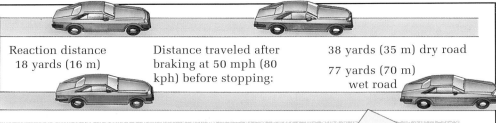

Reaction distance 18 yards (16 m)

Distance traveled after braking at 50 mph (80 kph) before stopping:

38 yards (35 m) dry road

77 yards (70 m) wet road

Action experiment

REACT!

Test your reactions with this experiment

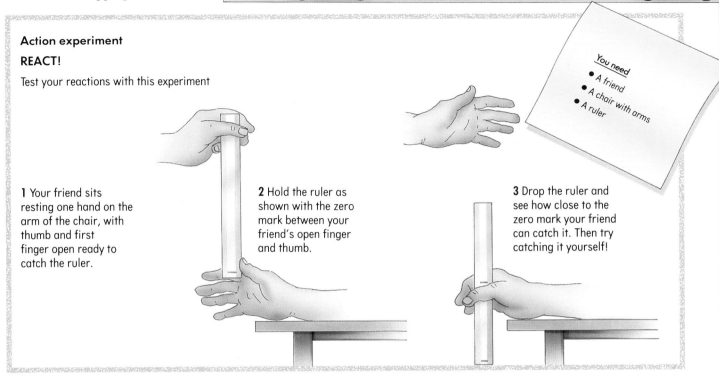

You need
- A friend
- A chair with arms
- A ruler

1 Your friend sits resting one hand on the arm of the chair, with thumb and first finger open ready to catch the ruler.

2 Hold the ruler as shown with the zero mark between your friend's open finger and thumb.

3 Drop the ruler and see how close to the zero mark your friend can catch it. Then try catching it yourself!

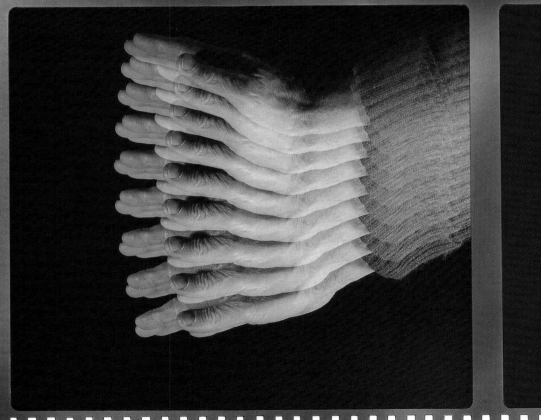

Your hand takes more than one tenth of a second to smack down.

Turning

When animals or objects turn, there is always a force trying to make them go forward in a straight line. The faster and tighter they turn, the stronger the force trying to make them go straight. When turning, an animal has to lean away from the force pushing it in a straight line. If it did not, it would fall over. The faster it turns, the more an animal must lean over. Birds and planes lean into their turns, for instance. This is called **banking**. Roads are made highest, or banked, at the outer curve of a bend. This helps to stop cars from rolling over and flying off the road when they corner at speed.

In a spin

As this amusement park rotor wheel spins around, you are pushed against its sides, like the marble in the bowl in the experiment on the right. At the top gravity pulls you downwards, but an equal force outward created by the spinning keeps you from falling in.

Going straight

Try whirling a ball on a length of string about 1 yard (1m) long around your head. The whirling ball wants to travel in a straight line but is pulled around by the string. The faster you whirl the more the ball pulls away from you and the harder you have to pull on the string to hold it back. If you let go of the string, the ball will fly off in a straight line, which is where it wants to go.

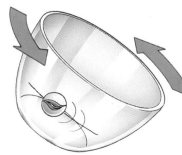

Put a marble into a bowl and make it whirl around. As it whirls faster, it climbs up the inside of the bowl. This is because it wants to go off in a straight line, like the ball on the string. But the sides of the bowl stop it from doing this, so it can only climb up instead.

This blue tit is banking as it turns after taking a peanut from a bird table.

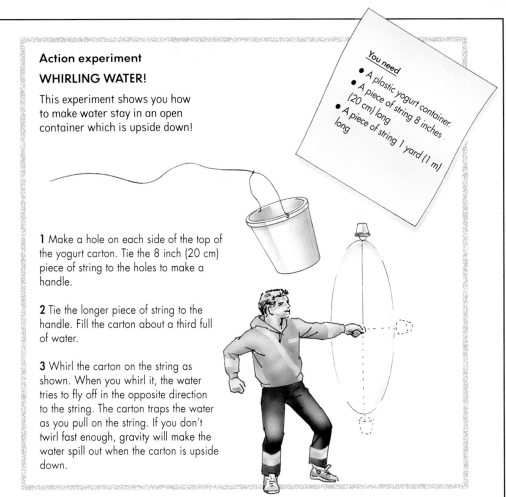
Leaning into the turn

Even when a dog, such as this collie, trots gently around a corner, there is a force trying to push it in a straight line. You can see how the dog has to lean over to counteract this. Racing motorcyclists lean over on the corners so much that their knees rub along the track.

Imagine trying to turn a corner on your bicycle without leaning over. Don't try it, or you could fall off and hurt yourself!

Did you know?

The Pendalino train in Italy tilts over as it goes around bends. This means that the train does not have to slow down very much at bends, which reduces the journey times.

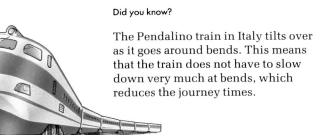

Stopping

If you drop a heavy brick into a sandpit, it will land with a thump and make a hole in the sand. Drop the brick on to an apple and it will squash it flat. The brick has **energy** because it is moving. When the brick stops suddenly, the energy has to go somewhere. It goes into the sand or the apple. The further the brick falls, the faster it moves and the more energy it has.

Putting on the brakes

When a pony stops suddenly, the rider goes on moving forward at the same speed and nearly goes over the pony's head!

Quick stop

If you drop an air gun pellet onto an apple nothing happens. But fired from an air rifle the pellet travels very fast and has lots of energy. This makes the apple explode when the pellet hits it.

ENERGY SPIDERS!

This experiment shows you how to make energy patterns.

1 Tape the pieces of cardboard together along the longest sides.

2 Fold the paper in half, open it and lay it with its fold along the taped join of the boards.

3 Soak the cube of sponge in paint and place it on the paper. Then carefully close the boards so that the sponge is sandwiched between the paper.

4 Fill the bag with sand and close the top with the elastic band. Drop it on to the closed boards holding the sponge.

Open the paper to see the energy spider made by the bag of sand. Experiment with different amounts of sand. You could try the same amount dropped from different heights. What differences can you see in the spiders?

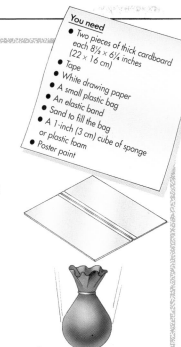

You need
- Two pieces of thick cardboard each 8½ × 6¼ inches (22 × 16 cm)
- Tape
- White drawing paper
- A small plastic bag
- An elastic band
- Sand to fill the bag
- A 1-inch (3 cm) cube of sponge or plastic foam
- Poster paint

Hammer that nail

Try pushing a nail into a piece of wood with your thumb. You cannot do it, can you? It needs a lot of energy to push a nail into wood. But if you hit the nail with a hammer, it goes in easily. The hammer stops suddenly when it hits the nail. Energy passes instantly to the nail and pushes it down into the wood.

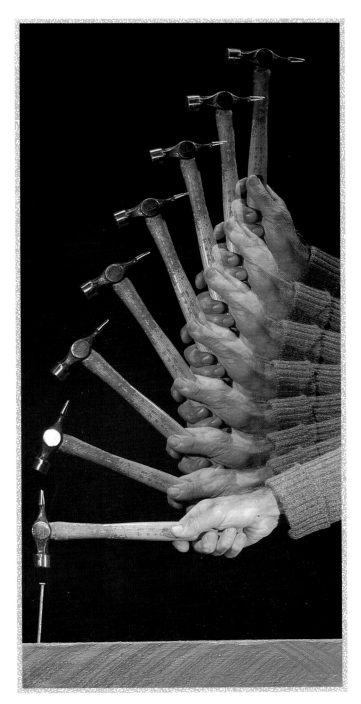

15

Crawling

Hundreds of millions of years ago, when animals first began to move about on the earth's surface, they could only crawl. Creatures with legs developed much later. A worm crawls by making the front part of its body long and thin, so that it stretches forward. Then the worm shortens and fattens its front part, hauling its tail towards its head so that its whole body is short and fat again. It is now ready to stretch forward once more. This is one of the earliest and simplest forms of crawling. Other animals, such as snails and snakes, have developed different styles of crawling.

Here you can see the bands of muscle on the snail's body. This garden snail has waves of muscle power moving from tail to head.

Muscle power

Crawlers need **muscle** power to move them along. A snake has muscles down each side of its body. When the muscles on one side contract, the body is pulled into a curve. A wave of muscle power then moves the curve down the snake's body. By pushing its curves against lumps in the ground, the snake moves itself along. Snails also use muscle power. A snail lays down a thin layer of slime on the ground and ripples its muscles so that it slides easily over the surface.

Did you know?

The largest land snail in the world is an African Giant snail. It is over 15 inches (38 cm) long and weighs about 2 pounds (900 g).

16

This grass snake is using curves in its body to push against stones so that it can move forward.

Action experiment

THE CRAWLER!

This experiment shows you how to make a simple "crawler".

1 Have an adult make a hole through the piece of candle with the scissors and cut a groove as shown. Thread the elastic band through the hole. Hold the band in place with a long matchstick laid in the groove.

2 Push the other end of the elastic band through the spool, and hold it with a piece of matchstick and a piece of tape. Wind up the elastic with the long matchstick, and the crawler will move along the floor or a table top.

Track power

The tracks on a caterpillar tractor are made up of steel bands which are linked together. As the tracks move over the ground, they push against stones, rocks, or earth. This makes the tractor move forward. Because the tracks are wide and long, they are much better than wheels for going over rough ground and climbing up very steep slopes.

Walking and running

Legs are better than wheels for traveling over rough ground. Humans and animals can adjust their strides to suit whatever kind of ground they are moving over. They dodge around, scramble or even jump over boulders and bushes in places where even a mountain bike would find it hard to go. The length of your stride depends on whether you run or walk, as the experiment below will show you. Legs are controlled by brain power, just like arms and fingers. (See page 10-11.)

Did you know?

The longest distance ever walked was by an American, Steven Newman, who walked around the world in four years.

Giraffes move differently from most other four-legged animals. When walking, they move both legs on the same side together.

Four legs

Most four-legged animals can trot, canter and gallop, as well as walk. When they walk or trot, they move a front leg with the back leg on the opposite side. A cantering animal has three feet off the ground at once most of the time. But all four feet are off the ground when an animal gallops.

Many legs

Animals with lots of legs, like this African millipede, move them in waves, otherwise they would get tangled up! Because of this, these animals cannot run. They can only walk quickly or slowly.

Two legs

There are two basic ways of moving along with two legs – walking and running. When walking, you always have at least one foot on the ground. A runner, like the one below, has both feet off the ground for some of the time. You never have both feet on the ground when running.

Action experiment

MEASURE YOUR STRIDES!

1 Measure out a distance of 20 yards (or 20 m) and mark the spot. First walk, then run the distance. Count the number of strides you take each time.

If you divide the distance of 20 yards (20 m) by the number of strides you take to walk or run, you will find out your stride length.

You need
- A tape measure
- A friend

Suppose you took 20 strides:

$$\frac{\text{Distance 20 yards (20 m)}}{\text{Number of strides 20}} = \text{1 yard (1 m) length of stride}$$

Jumping

All animals and humans have thick cords, like elastic, in their legs and arms which join the muscles to the bones. These cords are called **tendons**. Animals which jump, such as kangaroos, have long hind legs with very strong tendons. The tendons stretch a little each time the animal lands on the ground. The energy from landing is stored in the stretched tendon, ready to be used for helping with the next jump. These animals bounce along like rubber balls, using very little energy. Unlike them, frogs cannot bounce because they do not have such strong elastic tendons. Instead they hop, flopping down on their tummies, wasting all the energy of the jump.

Kangaroo

The hind legs of a kangaroo are very long and strong. It uses its thick, heavy tail to balance itself as it leaps through the air. The whole animal is specially shaped for jumping. Red kangaroos can jump a distance of over 13 yards (12 m), at a height of about 10 feet (3 m).

A common frog leaps to escape from danger.

Action experiment

FROG SURPRISE!

1 Cut this frog shape out of stiff cardboard. Then cut a slot as shown.

5 Twist the band two or three times, until it is tight.

2 Stick a piece of reusable adhesive underneath the frog's back legs.

4 When the elastic is tightly twisted, gently press the hairpin to the adhesive underneath the frog until it sticks.

3 Loop an elastic band around the frog and twist it with the hairpin.

5 The elastic band tries to untwist, and suddenly pulls the hairpin out of the adhesive, making the frog jump.

Frogs

A frog's legs are one and a half times the length of its body. Its long legs help the frog to jump distances of 20 inches (50 cm) or more. The greatest distance ever jumped by a captive frog in a competition was 11.3 yards (10.3 m)!

High jumpers

High jumpers use their tendons too. The record jump for women is 6 feet 10¼ inches (2.09 m) and for men 8 feet ½ inch (2.45 m).

Gliding and hovering

Did you know?

A monk named Eilmer made a 59 foot (18 m) hang glider flight from an abbey tower, 900 years ago!

If you hold a piece of paper level and drop it on to the floor, it will float down. This is because the flat surface of the paper pushes against the air and slows its fall. Many plants and birds use air like this. Dandelion seeds float along in the breeze and sycamore seeds spin down, slowed by a wing attached to them.

When air blows over hills, or is warmed, it rises. Gulls and gannets rest on rising air currents by spreading their wings flat. Hoverers, such as hawks and dragonflies, have to beat their wings rapidly in the still air to stay up, just as the rotor blades of a helicopter spin to keep it in the air.

The seeds of this goatsbeard plant float on the wind like parachutes.

Gliders

When the wind blows across the sea and hits a cliff, it is pushed upwards. This gannet does not have to flap to stay in the air. It stretches out its wings like a glider and rests them on the current of air being pushed up the cliff face.

Hoverers

This damselfly has two pairs of wings which flap in opposite directions. This means that it can hover, rather like a helicopter.

To make the helicopter hover, the pilot has to balance the lift of the big rotor with the push of the smaller tail rotor, so that the body of the plane stays still.

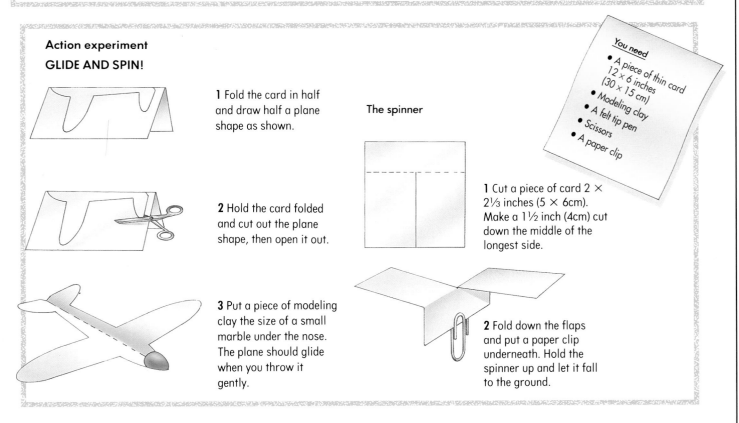

Action experiment
GLIDE AND SPIN!

1 Fold the card in half and draw half a plane shape as shown.

2 Hold the card folded and cut out the plane shape, then open it out.

3 Put a piece of modeling clay the size of a small marble under the nose. The plane should glide when you throw it gently.

The spinner

1 Cut a piece of card 2 × 2⅓ inches (5 × 6cm). Make a 1½ inch (4cm) cut down the middle of the longest side.

2 Fold down the flaps and put a paper clip underneath. Hold the spinner up and let it fall to the ground.

You need
- A piece of thin card 12 × 6 inches (30 × 15 cm)
- Modeling clay
- A felt tip pen
- Scissors
- A paper clip

25

Floating and skimming

The surface of water has an invisible layer on it like a skin. You can sometimes notice it when dust settles on a pond or puddle. Instead of sinking, the tiny grains of dirt rest on the water's skin. Though delicate, the surface skin of water is elastic, and springs back together if it is punctured. Small insects can ride and skim over the surface. Furry tufts on their feet break the surface and work like oars in the water to push the insect along.

This pond skater's feet make small depressions where they press into the surface of the water.

Water snail

Water snails, like this one, can cling underneath the surface skin of the water. When the snail lets go it may sink to the bottom.

Floaters

Water birds, such as ducks, swans, geese and gulls have oily feathers which repel the water. They smear oil from a gland on the top of their tails on to their feathers which then trap air, helping them to float like corks! Flying fish have fins like wings. They use the tips of their tails to send themselves skimming over the surface.

Skaters

Skating or skimming on the water is different from floating. Something that floats is partly below the surface, while a skimmer sits on top of the water. To do this an insect must be very light and **waterproof**, otherwise it would sink through the surface skin into the water below. Because oil is waterproof, surface skimmers have oily bodies and feet.

Did you know?

Flying fish glide over the surface at 35 miles (56 km) per hour, and can cover a distance of 153 yards (140 m) in 9 seconds!

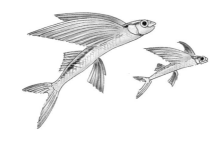

26

You need
- A needle
- A candle
- A bowl of water

Hovercraft

A hovercraft can skim over land or water. It has very powerful fans which blow air downwards. The air is trapped by a skirt and forms a cushion on which the hovercraft sits.

Swimming

Next time you have a bath, try a little experiment. Take a piece of card, about 6 inches (15 cm) square. Fold it in half and drag it through the water like a paddle. Now push it through the water, folded edge first. You will notice that the card slips through the water easily. This is because it is a **streamlined** shape. Something which is streamlined has a shape which makes very little water or air resistance (see pages 6-7). This is why most fish have slim, smooth bodies. Fish also have a slippery coating on their bodies which helps them to move more easily through the water.

Fins and flippers

A fish waves its tail from side to side when swimming. As it does so, the fish can bend its tail against the water and push itself forward. A swimmer's flippers work rather like this. They bend and press against the water when the swimmer kicks up and down. Fish use their side fins to guide them when they turn, dive and rise.

Did you know?

A sailfish can swim at over 60 miles (96 km) per hour, which is over 12 times faster than a person can swim.

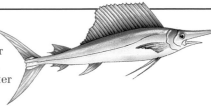

This rainbow trout bends its streamlined body as it turns, using its fins and tail to guide it around.

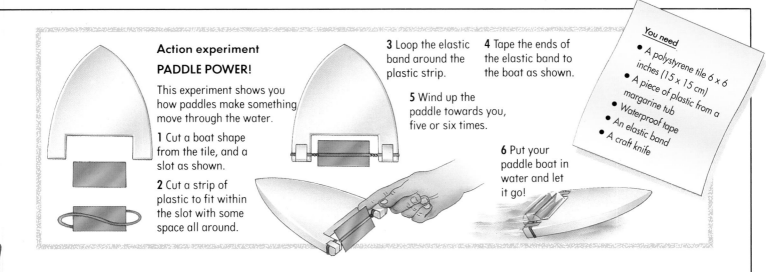

Action experiment
PADDLE POWER!

This experiment shows you how paddles make something move through the water.

1 Cut a boat shape from the tile, and a slot as shown.

2 Cut a strip of plastic to fit within the slot with some space all around.

3 Loop the elastic band around the plastic strip.

4 Tape the ends of the elastic band to the boat as shown.

5 Wind up the paddle towards you, five or six times.

6 Put your paddle boat in water and let it go!

You need
- A polystyrene tile 6 x 6 inches (15 x 15 cm)
- A piece of plastic from a margarine tub
- Waterproof tape
- An elastic band
- A craft knife

Wrigglers

A newt swims by wriggling its tail, which is flattened. The muscles in its tail make it bend like a snake's body, (see pages 16-17). The curves in the newt's tail press against the water, pushing it forward.

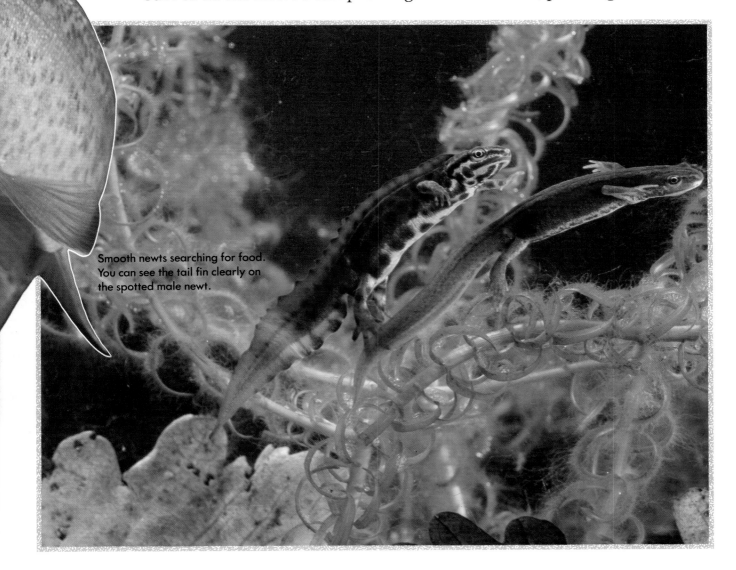

Smooth newts searching for food. You can see the tail fin clearly on the spotted male newt.

Jetting

No animal can jet along in the air. Only planes can do this. But some animals have been jetting along in the water for millions of years. These animals move by sucking in water then squirting it out very hard. The jet of water coming out in one direction pushes the animal along in the other. The simplest form of jetting is sucking in water and blowing it out through the same opening. Animals which are better at jetting have two openings: one for taking in water and the other for squirting it out.

Jet boats and jet planes

Jet ski boats use water to push them along, but really fast jet boats do not. They use the same sort of engines as jet planes. These engines suck in air and burn fuel in it. The burning fuel makes very hot gas which rushes out of the back of the engine. This pushes the boat forwards very fast.

Dragonfly nymph

A dragonfly nymph swims by jet **propulsion**. It sucks and blows water from one opening in its tail. Its progress is jerky as it nearly stops each time it sucks in water.

30

Pop-eyed squid

The pop-eyed squid has water intakes behind its head and a flexible jet **nozzle** underneath. It can cruise forward by pointing the nozzle backward. To escape from danger it points the nozzle forward and jets backward very fast.

Action experiment
JET POWER!

This experiment shows you how to make a simple kind of jet boat, using a balloon, and a piece of polystyrene tile.

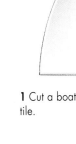

1 Cut a boat shape from the polystyrene tile.

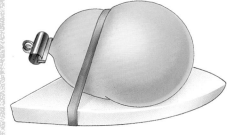

2 Blow up the balloon and close it with the spring clip. Tape the balloonn to the hull.

3 Place the boat in water and release the spring clip. The air will rush from the balloon and push the boat along.

Action words

Acceleration Speeding up, so that something goes faster and faster.

Banking Leaning over while turning.

Energy Power or force needed to move something or make something work.

Gravity The force that pulls objects back towards Earth.

Muscles The parts of a human or animal body that contract and relax to make the body move.

Nozzle A spout at the end of a tube, through which liquids can be pushed.

Propulsion Pushing something along.

Reaction The response to an action.

Speed The distance travelled in a known time.

Streamlined Shaped to pass more smoothly through air or water.

Tendons The strong cords in an animal's body that join the muscles to the bones.

Trajectory The path through the air taken by a freely moving object.

Vacuum Space without air.

Waterproof Having a surface that water cannot pass through.

Wing flaps Parts of an airplane's wings that can be moved to control the plane's flight.

Index